Conflict Tours

poetry by
Jonathan Travelstead

Copyright © 2017
ISBN: 978-1-941462-19-5
Cover by Caitlin Stoskopf
Book design by Andrew Keating

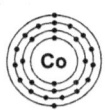

Cobalt Press
Billings, Montana

cobaltreview.com/cobalt-press

All rights reserved. No part of this book may be reproduced in any form, except for the inclusion of brief quotations in review, without written permission from the author/publisher.

For all inquiries, including requests for review materials, please contact cobalt@cobaltreview.com.

CONTENTS

Tourist

ONE

Field Worker
Simple
Letter to the Unborn
After a Tooth Extraction, Zen
Border Patrol
    In-Processing
    Riding the Beast
    Sonoran Desert. Warning by Rancher
    Corvids
    Flat Tire on San Miguel Road, Met by Two Wild Horses
    Injunction
    Money Tree, Detention Center
    Coyote

TWO

Ultralight
Complicated
Cartography
Rapture
Comfort
For Clothes
Trail Names
Myopia
Walasi-Yi Shoe Tree
Ridgerunner

THREE

Pleasure Principle (Pitbull Pills)
Scientist
Analysis Paralysis
Failure
Monster
Ghost

FOUR

Fission for Dummies
Pripyat
    Approach
    Schoolhouse
    Forest Wormwood
    Proximity
    ectopia cordis
    Signs
    Point and Shoot
    The Liquidators

FIVE

Education
Blue Chapel, Blue Cemetery
Petition
Addiction Tract
Pain of Others

Acknowledgments
About the Author

Conflict Tours

TOURIST

Gargoyles and fountains, patina-caked plaques
of monuments—you're quit with it. Three days now in the Czech Republic
and you've quit with journalling *I've seen so much significance I could puke*.
Quit with this shade of lonely which turns the noon hour
brown and yellow as if glassed on speed and espresso.

Then you, appending blurbs like solemn memes to posed,
digital photos taken by strangers. Your chin's stubbled thrust, blue eyes
squinting out-of-frame toward the crusade you make of concentration camps,
Prague Castle. The Klementinum. You marvel at the list of places
slashed with checks like an itinerary, or a set

of collector's Iron Man comics. Cavalier. Aloof,
you might be Bob Dylan, who never escaped a picture's centerstage.
A younger version, maybe, in that black-and-white, pre-electric poster,
bitchin' above your dorm room desk. As if it's something
you could even want once you knew the difference—

the traveller's persona lodged in your noodle like a soundtrack
for hand-me-down clones. When first did you risk an honest word? Geotagging,
then assigning emoticons to meals. Posting selfies where you're sipping
mulled wine at the Astronomical Clock's foot,
nursing another pint and the same damn book of poems

you read last night in a brick-arched tavern.
There is one liar in this poem and two musicians. I remember a hole
in the leather toe of a street violinist's wingtip shoes. I remember he played
"Wind Beneath My Wings," as I stood, planted in the middle of
Charles Bridge, remembering Bette Midler's version

against my mother's. Chest deflated, perilously near
a sob, I wanted espresso and a table. I wanted Wi-Fi to update my newsfeed
with a crafted loneliness I hoped strangers might mistake for bliss.
Then, home again, breaking my arm just to keep the string
pulled on the repeating track,

the one where you swear it's divine, you swear
you never wanted to leave—the one that says strangers are just relatives
to spirits our other lives forgot. Just another line saying Paris
is St. Louis where *yada yada yada* if a thing happens,
it always happens to you.

one

FIELD WORKER

All morning, bussed South from Mexico City,
Volkswagens and motorcycles caterpillared with three,
sometimes four riders blur by.

Blue smoke puffs from the chrome tailpipes,
a puttering exhaust indicating oil in the fuel, or worn rings,
neglected metal that will soon seize.

If angels breathe, they won't fly here.
Not where the Sierra Madres pierce the sky like ghosts
armored in beryl-horned caps, readying to march.

Not where the foreman breaks up groups of three or more
for fear of the men organizing.

Not in this place where a blight's thin, electric
green falls quiet from the slack sky, coating the sugar cane
with its fallout, or like Spring pollen.

My friend Oliver says the field workers die by the thousands
of a mystery kidney disease, but the owners say

pesos for a study would be a waste. Say *the workers
drink tequila*, say *they stay out late*, say *they only bring it
on themselves.* Oliver says his uncle chews

cane pulp instead of food, swings his machetes
through lunch. I've been on this bus too long not to care,

and so I mistake the low-flying crop-duster
for something holy when it glides by, streaming parathion,
paraquat in contrails from its wingtips,

which spreads over the men in a blue cloud
so you could believe the cane is harvested by the dead.

§

Black apron, blue hat. Golden arches
instilling feelings of expansion, escape from poverty
through the Gateway to the West.

Sixteen. Weekends at McDonald's working midnights.
Safety First. On a Friday after closing, the manager snuck his girlfriend
into the office, tossed out a package of scouring acid
kept in a lockbox, then shut and locked the door.

I wanted the Material Safety Data Sheets,
but he told me *quit bein' such a pusssy*, so I went back to clean the grill.
Hunching so I couldn't see my reflection in the one-way mirrors
or the truth of what happens behind them, the lemony fluid
squished in my fingers like a melted *Icee Pop*.

I didn't read the directions, but when I tore the package open
with my teeth the acid splashed my hands with lesions,
ghosting them with scars months after.

§

What my great-grandfather said about working coal seams
for scrip—the stamped-out copper coins used in the company store
in place of money. *They gave us shit and called it sunshine.*

Years he passed from one twelve-hour night to another. In a way,
I think I can see him, emerging from a hole
coughing plumes of coal dust the mucker mucked onto him,

wiping the black into a slurry which filled the creases of his face.
My eyes open again on the fields, and I see hours when minutes
are all we have, field workers trading

the only precious thing they have for what settles in the hands
before reaching their lungs, their family. I see the working dead.
Grandfathers and children alike, their leathery hands

rasping beads up the bolos of straw hats. I see loose pants, chambray.
I see helmets where rust has settled into the dents put there
by clinkers. I see spit-carbide lanterns.

Mouths the earth's insides have permanently drawn down.
I see them grilling tamales at the back of bicycle carts. I see the field
and the poor bastards in them hobbling bundles of cane

to rusted beds of pickups like a trolley of mining cars.
The short lives we live. The work we do not because it's what we want,
but because we believe we must.

SIMPLE

I stoop in the market between slatted bins
of guava, coffee-skinned Belizeans, and when I correctly
name a black-haired girl's puppy

perro, she smiles, tucks into my hand a flat piece of jade.
The gift: flecked with chips of pale green.
There could be no other like it, and because it is easier

choosing the world we want to see,
I watch light-footed women move expertly beneath
baskets of textiles, melons balanced evenly

on Hellenic heads. Their breasts hustle them
down the pitched streets in linens the color of a robin's
eggshell, tunics purple as the pitaya's neon flesh.

Black beans a woman doles out to me on a fry jack
from her tortilla cart.

§

It was all so romantic I almost believed the fables
of a singular enlightenment which enables a welfare recipient
to turn luxury away. I almost believed I could deny

the white gods who decloud on the eighth day, proffering fire
in the form of smartphones, and management positions
at Volkswagen assembly lines, sugar refineries.

That they could again be rejected after their second coming
in the scrubs of plastic surgeons, promising silicone
like clear jewel for women's lips so they could be

more like Angelina Jolie's.
                             Of course none of that happens,
or ever does. Even I want to look like Angelina Jolie.

Saints don't retire to the tropics, subsisting on bread alone
as they comb the white sands for peace. Nobody refuses
gigabit wireless, turning back instead to the fields

where harvesting cane sprains the back righteously out of alignment.
Waiting for the silver-backed apes to descend bearing gifts
of minimum wage, overages with two year contracts,

I, too, want abundance in the form of another zed added
to my surname's right side. Who doesn't want what overflows
the outstretched hand—jade or a vermilion paper

soluble enough we can make it rain? *I want. More,*
the burden of saying I would kill just to keep.

LETTER TO THE UNBORN

To David

The first and only time I hunted deer, my father and I holed up
in an old Ford van rusted in the runners.
Unupholstered rear doors flung open to woods,
we kindled ourselves with the secrets between us.

Cocoa with butterscotch Schnapps. Limericks.
I admitted skipping even numbers of railroad ties,
once chunking granite onto a killdeer nest between the tracks.

Puffs of pent-up breath as our crosshairs swayed,
searching for Bambi. Steam and snow and what he said:
Don't name what you intend to kill.

To Katherin

Head against the glass of the bus, I wake.
Remember Belize. Clay beyond the face staring back at me,
gravel-sluiced and bleeding.

Today I paid a local Mayan to show me what is,
what could have been.
Wild poinsettias, rubber trees lined the path.
Howler monkeys monitored our progress.
Shrieked from one breadfruit tree
to the next.

The guide showed me the rappelling gear,
how an unclenched fist lets you descend to the blue spring
where we swim beneath stone, come up
in a cave's darkness.

There, a child's bones, sacrifice.
Her lithified skeleton splayed, face-down in my head lamp's light.
I see where the rib broke. I see, too, the groove
where a spear's flint notched her spine,
where her father's hands entered, retrieved her heart.

To Katherin or David

What majority vote did I have
deciding against your possibility between two pink lines,
the woman I loved?

Yolk-glazed, flecked with coffee grounds,
I keep your names I liked best in a lockbox on a cancelled check
riffled from the trash days after the procedure.

On the check's back, a stick child in a woven basket.
Scrawled in carbon copy beneath two columns of names,
their meanings, circled in red.

Beloved, Innocent.
You are, and I think of you each time I travel,
finding you again as artifacts ghosting the windows of buses,
trains, or laid away deep in a secret cave.

David, or Katherin,
if there were any lessons I could have given you
remember these two things:
Love your mother,
and know it is easier to be the one who leaves
than it is to be the one left behind.

AFTER A TOOTH EXTRACTION, ZEN

Sometimes it is good not giving a shit.
Vicodin. Red Solo cup of flat, frothy beer.
A clove's smoke threading from your knee
as you watch through steel bars.
In San Juan, barefoot, lopsided boys
crack ball-valves at the rear of bus coaches,
one-arming five gallon buckets of waste
to the weeds. We are not our thoughts—
just empty vessels in frequent need
of being emptied, aired out. Glass jewels
the hostel wall in green shards
and remnants of clear bottles like rock candy
or the gila's brittle teeth. As if through
water, in slow motion, cabbies crash taxis
on curbs, then flap their jaws, nattering.
Numb. Blissful. Ask if I even care.

BORDER PATROL, ARIZONA

In-processing. Sunnyside High School, Tuscon

The square-jawed sergeant snatches my orders.
*Nothing that matters burns here. Congratulations, Airman First Class—
You're a medic.* Shunts me to a female private beneath
the basketball hoop who, with an IV and an orange bruised soft as skin,
instructs me on the military's care towards aliens.
Cups my hand clasping the orange in hers. Finds the sweet spot in four
or less punctures. Suddenly it's my lone hand which holds the fruit.

My hand puncturing its rind with eighteen gauge holes
   like pinpoint windows that unlatch from the inside because in battle
the only *I believe in* that matters is attendance, why minutes later
   I'm burdened beneath kevlar, a helmet two wars old and missing
its lining. Topographic maps of dusty cattle-roads (useless after first washout)
   winged under one arm. Under the other, orders amended
with signatures certifying my crude proficiency in Tex-Mex,

   the Law of Armed Conflict, rules of engagement briefings,
and a crash course in medical training to include intubation on all things
   American. America. Where the line items qualifying
for participation include *1) Warm Body*, and *2) My Parents Fucked Here*.
   Only now the barefaced, double butterbar lieutenant
marches from the bivouac of a coach's office to this know-nothing airman
   planted at attention beneath the free throw line.

Exchanges salutes of diplomatic importance, reciting phonetically
   from an index card, each word a sharp-edged stone tumbled, slicing
at the thin flesh in his mouth: *Como fway to entry nameento?*
   Remember, it's only a boy there after all, *un pequejo hijo*
who squeaks as the keys to a medic's Humvee line-and-tackle plop
   into his outstretched hand. Backboard projecting, askew,
from the canvas flap in the rear. Tylenol. Cases of Gatorade's

yellow electrolyte gruel we dare not ask whose hands—
in what Latin country's assembly line—have filled and capped. This shining,
   newly-christened Grand Poobah of Sonora's mesas
will pilot the street cleaner of our dusty back alleys. This cherub
   in camouflage pampers will stitch together our border's serrated lines.

Riding the Beast

The yellow Union Pacific locomotive blows,
chuffs a ragged line from Tapachulas through Chiapas, then El Norte.
Immigrants shake sleep from their eyes,
the thousand aches where flint dented their backs
through blankets soiled black,
left for them alongside the tracks.

They vault when the train passes through
shoe-soles flapping like dessicated tongues,
lance themselves to its flank.

Some fall, forgetting to close their hands
around the rust-flecked rungs.
Some drop cornhusk tamales from canvas packs
as they shoot up the ladders like cucarachas
to two square feet on the train's steel-trussed roof
they make signs of the cross that they will keep.

  §

In Benton I buy peaches
from a farmer for whom illegals pick fruit at three dollars an hour.
He insults them, then confides

no one educated enough for English picks
in the upper branches

then,

a hundred chalupas atop a train car is a family portrait,
but when a train car slices into a low-slung tunnel
it's a damn good start

  §

My three-times-great grandmother
Magritha Catherine Uhle wrote in her leather diary
how she tossed forty days in the hold of a sailing ship
from Hamburg to Castle Gardens.
Just before reaching mainland, sailors
threw over the typhus-pocked bodies
bound together with sisal rope.

They came apart like sheaves of paper in the scalloped waves.

The next entry she strolled into Manhattan
and this new country, diary clasped in one hand, an orange
flickering from the other.

    §

How hard it must be to give your life to the ship holds
the way aliens give theirs to the tops of train cars—
boys and women routinely raped,
failing to palm over mordidas for protection against police
and bandits who exchange titles like silver-tipped bolos.

Stories too unpalatable for telling over coffee,
they're just one more thing in a ticker tape of trivialities which happened
but won't make the entertainment news
that won't blare down the tracks of your living room
a thing that won't make the tailgates of peach farmers.

Who doesn't want to sleep deeply,
made safe if only by the closeness of someone who loves them?

They daisy-chain themselves one to another with hemp
beneath a sky's boxed lid gouged with holes instead of stars,
then pray they don't slip between the linkages
in the engine's rock and rumble.
If they do, then at least they go together
to the creosote ties and the wheels and the stones.

If they do, no one that is not there will look back
as it chews the wings, the chitinous shells from their blessed bodies.

Sonoran Desert; Warning by Rancher

Look West from the cattle fence.
Bulkheads front-run the approaching storm.
Smoke, three hundred miles out
hangs above Los Angeles county's wildfires
like a knot's thirteenth turn, or an elk hide scraped clean,
tanned in potash.

Thunderheads spark hidden places in steel wool
you never guessed and cannot see.

The papers say you only have to look South to see the black tide.

Beautiful dark-haired women from Los Zetas.
Cartels from Juarez who would as soon hack off your head as look at you.
That smell riding the wind? Job loss, *Undocumented Aliens*
entering our home through our ragged fences, children.

Any man believes that is a fool.

Feel it now, your chest quicken
at the white skirl of cotton flitting there between stripped
Chevy Suburbans and Ford SUVs long ago scudded to a stop in dust,
dessicated frames driven as far as momentum
and bare rims allow.

At the border, two bodies like estranged lovers meet,
bone dry as a snap of light matches its clatter. A raindrop craters hardpan.
A deluge breaks between chaparral and prickly-pear,
flooding the arroyo and any way home.

Fear strains your eyes as saguaro walk on the water.
See how fear makes even the cacti fugitive,
posed, mid-flight.

Corvids

Want to catch a crow? Study the alien, its shiny things. Foil hat.
Mirrors, chewing gum wrappers wadded in nests.
Three hundred million years since our species parted ways.

Them, closer to the lizard brain than the smartphone's halo.
From straws watch them make tools.
Pincer strips of raw beef through dowel. Solve riddles

requiring eight steps of critical thinking. Watch as this crow
plinks pebbles in a glass until water displaces a pistachio
within reach of the rim. They're crafty.

Half the presidential hopefuls say we should take back
the good names we gave them. They're smart. Peppered with shot,
a change in route and elevation gets passed on to the next crew.

Screen a dome over the tomatoes, watch their scouts
well-practiced miming the killdeer's portrayal of a broken wing
skirt your garden while a murder tunnels the fence.

I've heard tell blackberry pies vanish from windows.
Sheets nicked from clothespins, Flagstaff to Portland. Canadian
ice fishermen drop lines into sawed holes, later report a mess

of nylon and trout scales, feathers spaghettied in snow.
Crow, rook. Blackbird, raven. I heard a story once say Noah's ark
might contain the hummingbirds' names, but I'm not sure.

In oh-four I broke down in Roswell and one showed me
how to bridge my solenoid's broken circuit with a flat-head.
They say each can do the job of ten men.

They say they don't think like we do.
They don't need much.

Flat Tire on San Miguel Road, Met by Two Wild Horses

Take your broken carriage and go.
We have documented your arrivals
Have taken your Humvee into account
Among desert scrub and sage.
Your rumbling wakes the land
Disturbs gila from their secret dens.
Nothing knows where it is born
In what parched land it will awaken
When the Rio Grande says to the sky
"Sky, today I will go this other way."
Pale stranger with your pain bodies
Your own enlistments of mercy
Tell me who you are to draw a line
Our myths cannot cross

Injunction

PFC Moreno and I rumbled through Sells,
then onto the cattle road which wound around the mountain to the lookout post.
A mile out and we could see the soldiers and airmen there,
camouflaged behind DayGlo orange netting.
Everyone could see them. On the lookout for aliens
with their playing cards and white sunblock, laptops and DVDs.

We had just begun trundling the steep grade,
where closer to its weathered top the Humvee would lose purchase,
clattering on stones and flat spots
before grabbing dust and lurching forward.
I was almost lost in the paint of that scene when a Mexican
stepped out of the dry, thin air in front of the cattle guard,
flagging us down.

He was shirtless, in a white raffia hat.
Moreno understood better than I—his wife nearby, unconscious.
Moreno radioed that our engine had overheated
but that we had bottled water
so no one would come looking. We found Maria
where he showed us, keeled against a green metal table
sympathizing Indians from the Tohono Reservation weekly resupplied
with jugs and bleach bottles of good water.

The same water which lay slashed and boot-stomped in the dust.

I remember the jet-black of her hair, hung
like the buckshot-peppered rags of rattlers strung over barbed wire.
The rasp of her moistureless breath,
shoulders rising in fits and starts.

I may never learn how to say this,
how sometimes the Great Divide is not a landmark
so much as the boundary
where you decide between giving more than regulations permit
and how much sleep you need at night.

A wet towel and water.
An orange he kneaded in cracked hands,
punctured with his thumbs, then split apart
like opening a book to its middle.

Directions.
Cancelled radio traffic.
A finger, pointing two clicks North.

Money Tree, Border Patrol Detention Center

Dropping their bills beneath the tree
so as to not be identified by their home countries,
captured immigrants file inside for processing.
Soon, in fiat pastels, Latin royalty
lie clovered beneath the twisted canotia.
Benito Juarez. Christopher Columbus. Jose Maria.
I believe I see humanity also
behind the agents' drab khakis and aviators
who look away from the queue of aliens
as they shed colons and quetzales,
American dollars dug up at arranged locations,
nationalities wadded like love notes
from dying countries.

Coyote

On a mesa near Tohono
we chock the Humvee's wheels with sharp stones,
then watch for an hour through binoculars as the broad-shouldered native
wearing black sweats walks two miles South to the silver bullet trailer
crowding Mexico's side of the cattle fence.
Cut in the makeshift taco stand a lone two-by-four
props the hinged plywood awning
so in its shadow we can't confirm the exchange of routes
or patrol times. Watching them,
stark against our mountain,
I wonder what secrets one must think they know
to play custodian to a country. The Mexican hands him a Corona,
then chorizo in a wrapper made clear by grease.
Finished, the Native American
collars another by its neck, staggers, then wheels back,
stumbling on the first rut, passing out cold,
drunk on the little he had been given
in the cattle road's dust.

two

ULTRALIGHT

The mess kit—a threaded aluminum silver disk:
two pans fastened together (two-hundred fifty grams)

Silver pot (eighty-five grams, ten removed by angle grinder)
Cellophane bag of powdered eggs (ninety, vaccuum-sealed by mouth)
Black spatula, blade ground, handle filed (one-fifty)

Stove: Two beer can bottoms, slit, then sleeved together—
five holes needled to a star's shape

Fuel: One yellow bottle of *Heet!* carburetor cleaner

Hammock, rainfly: a cinched fist (eight-hundred)
Rock salt kneaded into beeswax, molded into a lip balm tube (thirty-nine)
Titanium outline: blue tanto, drilled and machined hollow (sixty-two)

    §

My clothes, moisture-wicking.
Iodine for water. Isopropyl for fire.

Dyneema. Polypropylene. Sil-nylon, capilene, and silicon.

Materials reduced to their properties propel me
through Neal's—and Hogspen Gap, the Blue Ridge Mountains.
Where there are walls I carve doorways.

Closed, I clutch the blade
dangling loose from the slipknot on my chest strap—
less than a kilo of pull and it's freed. Bumps
tumoring my hip-belt pocket.
Adderall. I know where everything is,
exactly how much I carry.

COMPLICATED

> To make a deep mental path, we must think over and over
> the kind of thoughts we wish to dominate our lives.
> —Henry David Thoreau

It should be simple,
but, three days north from the Amicalola trailhead
and he still can't lose himself in the nomenclature of trees
for this cataloguing of what is carried
against what is needed:

Bic razor. At the next town crossing he'll toss it,
and with it any need for a stream's reflection. His chest straps dangle,
useless as dewclaws, so he cuts them as if loosening ballast.

Indebted to the orange pitbull pills
as if they saved his life and he is now responsible for them—
they lock his jaw and attention to the white-blazed trees
beside the narrow, dished-out trail.
What once helped him look inward when a woman
he loved would come home, her mouth balled into fists.

He hears the diamondback's rattle,
a tintinnabulum in dry leaves against occupying the past.
He hears Thoreau's whisper that each man's burden
possesses him, draws even his eyes inward.

He toils the switchbacks and ridgelines,
imploring the summit for a brief reprieve between complications,
the ragged half-breath of presence he calls freedom.

It should be simple, he thinks.
Eat. Hike. Sleep. What he means: *Be your last breath.*

CARTOGRAPHY

Weeks whistle by in the Chattahoochee and Nantahala Forest
and all you have is this shadowbox of mountains, balds, and gaps:

Hawk, and Springer. Gooch,
Tray, Cowrock, and Blue. Blood Mountain—
where you watched from the shelter a black bear
solve your trucker's hitch, snuffling your food across roots,
the stamped-down path, taking nothing.

Balds. Siler, Wayah, and Wesser. Swim, and Cheoh.

Gaps, flat points where mountains meet
like pauses between ascending and descending notes:

Hightower, Horsebone, and Flatrock.
Unicoi. Mooney, Glassmine, and Tesnatee.
Winding Stair, and Swinging Lick.
Panther. Licklog, Burningtown, and Tellico.
Simp, Stecoah, and Sweetwater.
Cable, and Black Gum.

You can only name the sweet music of each step.
Scribbled crossings, summits,
and roundabouts of a musician exploring the scales,
but not so lost he can't take a bearing
by mouthing a landmark alone.

RAPTURE

The pitbull voice says
Take this, my capsule, its orange and clear ends
unsleeved for you, and come up

in remembrance of me.
The addict's tongue. Pasty, Dreamsicle-orange with
bitter amphetamine salts. Iris flare,

the sunlight falling. Hummingbird
nested in the space between ribs. Your last thought,
you are it, sustained forever.

O Benzedrine, Dexedrine.
O cold blue angel of methylphenidate, Concerta, and Ritalin—
I hum with praise, I hum with joy,

I hum blind, cordant glory in threading
octaves. I hum a stream of confessions overflowing their banks.
I am many acolytes speaking,

an army of tongues. I am the fleet-foot's
quickened step. Forgiveness for transgressions against me
I've already forgotten. I lift (hosannas)

these tongues to the frequency and strata
of endless accomplishment and unrequited acquisition I lift this euphoria
of title and order and gain in dumb, narcotic bliss.

(please hear me in the parentheses,
this hosanna's fevered plea that it pierce obsession)
Bless this gritty ambrosia for me and only me,

(O, power, save me from this pitbull focus,
this verbal masturbation) and I ask that you lift me faster higher
longer in your glory

(God save this rat trapped in the sugar stores Amen)

COMFORT

The legless camp chair made of nylon
which rolls up and weighs only five-hundred grams.

Jokers removed, a deck of cards
you bored quarter-sized holes through with a Forstner bit.

The plastic cross perforated with grids your sister crocheted
in green- and salmon-colored yarn.

Eye-dropper of dish soap.

Wool shirt, alpaca.

Pizza. Mushroom, garlic, extra sauce.

These are the things you don't pack
for their poor calorie-to-weight ratios, for how
pleasure softens also the body.

What you have:
Two lines of James Kimbrell's "Mount Pisgah,"
The Doxology inked on your forearm.

Old Crow whiskey, one liter.

For how it dehydrates the body but wets also your eyes
so you feel something, so you might finally deserve such comfort.

FOR CLOTHES

Fifty feet off the trail in a low valley, afternoon.
Nude. Ankle-hunched, dips his clothes in moving water.

The fold in his belly tells him he is aging.
His penis withdraws from the warning of cold water below,
as if seeing a fish or its reflection for the first time.

There is no such thing as silence.

He knows this, and so takes the bare blade of the razor
from its taped sleeve. Wrings his only clothes out in the stream,
slings them over his pack to dry.

Because some things won't scale away,
because tension and release are the silence that never was
but still he tries, he shoulders his pack, still naked,

earth padding his soles brown and gritty.

Maple-shadow and oak dapple his face, body.
White sarvis blossoms catch his shoulder.
Stick to his wet, chafing thighs.

TRAIL NAMES

If we named one another for qualities of nature, a title might conjoin the thickness
of a tree's bough with a wild panther. I think of the Cherokee and Sewanee
who scattered as Paul Bunyan cleared the Smokies. I think of the boast
of tall tales and of Bones, a surly northbounder with us tonight in this fire tower,

who charts by laser pointer in the night sky potential earths, where it is
he thinks we're going. Someone should tell John Wayne tomorrow—swaggering
into view on the switchback of an eastern-facing ridge, boonie hat pinned,
pemmican offered from the tip of his bowie knife. Strangers clothed

in characters we find familiar. Sore and sacked out by the Nolichucky River,
Captain Jack shakes my hammock awake, gives me a snort from his flask
for the blessing of good company. Tonight, the campfire makes us feel
we're getting away with something in naming our lonesomeness. Nowhere Man,

and his friend, Lone Wolf, flickering faces. Middle-aged, single. One an accountant,
the other on Wall Street, each naming themselves for traits they desire most,
glancing in the glow of each face as if waiting for meaning's arrival.
Tonight we shelter in beans and ramen. In Big Country—the bottomless Georgian

who annexes leftovers and unwanted equipment into his sixty-pound pack.
Noodles. Tent stakes, though I don't remember his tent. Maybe we do in this way
share a kinship with what lived here before, sharing everything we can,
then christening ourselves with allegories which dismantle even good,

strong fences. An Illinois hiker claims a black bear cub waits ahead on the trail
where a blitz of red wattle and a blur of black wings dub him Turkeybear.
Wasabi Pea. Blonde, every twenty steps or so you can hear cellophane, then *crunch*!
so she doesn't smoke. How many more names like credits scrolling after a film

before the web of characters is visible? How long before I open my mouth again
and give the premonition flesh, admit I've known them my whole life,
but only just met? Nip Slip, Floats, and Clean Cut. Bike Cop, C-Biscuit.
Ain't Got One. Toots.

MYOPIA

Careful in keeping to the path,
my headlamp splashes a blue slab of splintered pine fallen across the deertrack.
Blazed neon with fungus, a salamander flames over,

spiralling the trunk with golden slashes stippled down its back.
Particles of light escape my field of vision where a white birch flashes silver
to my left. Enough moon, I click off my torch. Fireflies.

Only a few at first. Sporadic, this species twitters
as if strung on the same circuit which is flicked on, then off. On.
Emeralds, or maybe bits of broken bottle glint among needles

at the forest floor. Where I expect only dew
jewelled on the bladed tips of grass, I chase them to their source.
Each time, a spider's eyes glinting my wonder back to me,

more treasure I'd been missing all this time,
just out-of-frame, just off the path.

WALASI-YI SHOE TREE

for Heidi

Not thirty miles North of the approach trail where we cross Neel's Gap
and the highway, failure and victory dangle in the branches of a single tree.

Southbounders just completing the trail, Northbounders, or quitters who up
and decide they've had enough return here years later so they can sling

their busted sneakers, broke-strapped sandals, or boots like bolas
until they catch and twine the low-hanging branches, their trail names

scrawled in the soles. You've seen something like them near your home,
straddling telephone lines, out of reach, though it didn't mean the same thing.

Here among leaves, laces and aglets hang like stringers of bluegill,
or sunfish. Couched in yokes where two branches meet, flapping soles

twinned with *Turkeybear*, or *Wasabi Pea*, their script a dead-ringer
for its mate. Always in pairs, you think of lovelocks on a bridge in Italy

with the woman you love who you believe loves you. Together,
you rolled the stainless shank over the Master Lock's tumblers and tossed

the key off the foot trail in La Spezia. You think also of the lyric
Should I stay or should I go and promises made between animated canines

having a Disney moment over pasta. Nothing is assured but two loops,
and spooled linguini. Nothing but this knot of time saying, *Yes, we were here.*

RIDGERUNNER

It's a solitary process, and the user prefers using alone. Adrenaline,
oxygen sifted in the correct ratio. The runner's high scored by hurdling solitude
to the body's pleasure-rattle. Cortisol, endorphins.
So many ways to self-medicate, our sweet tooth draws us
towards the ache we mistake for bliss.
His: twenty miles so he can champion Unicoi by noon,
then Standing Indian Mountain by dusk. He doesn't believe
expiration dates or that he can die. Afraid any slowing in pace
is the same as standing still,
he moves as if inertia might evade the question
skimming beneath the surface. Whatever he says is true,
if only because saying makes it so. *Am I worth stopping for?*
Serotonin, enriched atmospheres
prevent the question's flicker into speech.

All color and pulse, the Crayola forest of trees blur
where lime meets alpine. Blasting through his second wind, he believes
elevation lightens each step to nirvana
like a firework bursting into sparks on his eyelids' back
as he touches himself again, and won't let anyone,
anything, touch him.

WALASI-YI SHOE TREE

for Heidi

Not thirty miles North of the approach trail where we cross Neel's Gap
and the highway, failure and victory dangle in the branches of a single tree.

Southbounders just completing the trail, Northbounders, or quitters who up
and decide they've had enough return here years later so they can sling

their busted sneakers, broke-strapped sandals, or boots like bolas
until they catch and twine the low-hanging branches, their trail names

scrawled in the soles. You've seen something like them near your home,
straddling telephone lines, out of reach, though it didn't mean the same thing.

Here among leaves, laces and aglets hang like stringers of bluegill,
or sunfish. Couched in yokes where two branches meet, flapping soles

twinned with *Turkeybear*, or *Wasabi Pea*, their script a dead-ringer
for its mate. Always in pairs, you think of lovelocks on a bridge in Italy

with the woman you love who you believe loves you. Together,
you rolled the stainless shank over the Master Lock's tumblers and tossed

the key off the foot trail in La Spezia. You think also of the lyric
Should I stay or should I go and promises made between animated canines

having a Disney moment over pasta. Nothing is assured but two loops,
and spooled linguini. Nothing but this knot of time saying, *Yes, we were here.*

RIDGERUNNER

It's a solitary process, and the user prefers using alone. Adrenaline,
oxygen sifted in the correct ratio. The runner's high scored by hurdling solitude
to the body's pleasure-rattle. Cortisol, endorphins.
So many ways to self-medicate, our sweet tooth draws us
towards the ache we mistake for bliss.
His: twenty miles so he can champion Unicoi by noon,
then Standing Indian Mountain by dusk. He doesn't believe
expiration dates or that he can die. Afraid any slowing in pace
is the same as standing still,
he moves as if inertia might evade the question
skimming beneath the surface. Whatever he says is true,
if only because saying makes it so. *Am I worth stopping for?*
Serotonin, enriched atmospheres
prevent the question's flicker into speech.

All color and pulse, the Crayola forest of trees blur
where lime meets alpine. Blasting through his second wind, he believes
elevation lightens each step to nirvana
like a firework bursting into sparks on his eyelids' back
as he touches himself again, and won't let anyone,
anything, touch him.

three

PLEASURE PRINCIPLE (PITBULL PILLS)

Eight-fifteen. In bed, I crunch the capsule, grind the orange spheres
between my teeth, bitter as early walnut. Twenty-seven minutes
on an empty stomach and the fluorescents thrum like light sabers.

My body splits its calyx, rising into them, radiant as the drug's pathway
from *sub lingua* to reptilian brain, then flutter of chest,
a didgeridoo's single vowel. Resonates through pectoralis major,

pronator teres. *Om.* Light as down, I come up beneath a loaded flat bar.
Bend my torso forward in the exercise called 'good mornings'.
Snatch-and-clean until my hams and glutes are depleted uranium,

napalm jelly quivering in the place of legs. If anyone else is here
I don't see them, jaws tetanic, thrust into presence by pain of
each repetition. Soundtrack of clanging, dropped plates.

Nothing pierces the hum of the pitbull sergeant's voice, his glottal *UP!*
DOWN! How long has he been here? Skull crushers until
the pincered dumbbell swells my triceps like a radial tire about to blow,

frayed steel belt herniating. Shoulders tight as a funeral procession,
I unrack, and piston cast iron, blood rising in blue distributions
over my arms. Servant. Always the engine, never the engineer.

Trembling with the *pump* or exhaustion—I don't know which—
I remember someone appeared, helped guide me back to the hooks.
My vision returned in blots, with it my lust after the pyramid of failure,

recovery. Drop weight. Again.

SCIENTIST

Barefoot, he appears sculpted
as if from slabs of clay, hand-chucked onto rebar.
The bodybuilder's intake of breath:
A vacuum priming cobalt from his veins

for his transition from a side chest
to back double biceps position he strains in the mirror
until he sees a body in it, lithic with blood.
Each day he dissects himself as he dissects you,

studying supersymmetry between calories
counted in oat flake and egg yolk.
A measured eight hours of sleep so muscle can devise
new methods for bluffing the dumb bell.

Scar beautifully toward the golden ratio.
In remembrance of his gods—Arnold, and Lou—
he stands in effigy, sheened in oil,
gnarled sinew torqued from the hoist and heave

in calculated angles against gravity.
Sometimes, he feels the back-breaking weight
of the ascetic's life. No tolerance
for touch between iron and the notebook's cold ledger.

In the mirror a little boy tightens his diaphragm.
Curls a beach ball, shows you the beach.
Still, you cannot look away. Nothing in his intercostal
landscape can be plucked

and still allow for equal measure.

ANALYSIS PARALYSIS

A quick in-and-out and nobody gets hurt, you promise,
popping a sleeved capsule before walking into
the Kroger's. Only suddenly
it's two-oh-five
and you've been fingering packages
of meat on Manager's Special for fifteen minutes
comparing orange stickers on sirloin.
Quality, in terms of fat marbling,
sodium, firmness
when pinched. Weighing options among the gray
and the cast aside. Cellophane-wrapped
chuck two days shy of expiration,
muscle's destiny
decided by arbitrary numbers. What time is it?
Put the package down. Check your phone. Ten minutes,
you told yourself. Return to the lonely
and the rifled-through
preserved in plastic-foam platters.
This one—void of the red dye injected for the illusion
of blood. See how it sponges into foam backing
with the tiny, diagonal
imprints sandwiched between polystyrene
and plastic. What time is it? Exchange the container
for one whose price is digitally stamped
on the yellow tag.
Three for three. Nearly a dollar a pound.
Can that be right? Weight, divided by cost, or cost
multiplied by net weight? There's an app
for that. Phone.
Make necessary calculations.
Check email. Facebook. Thank you, no, the penis pills
didn't work the first time. Pocket phone,
forget to check time and figure,
but now floaters dance

like amoebae across your vision, alphanumeric symbols
unwinding as they hike across the label,
mountainous over beef.
A word said thirty times loses
its meaning's hard edges, lies dumb on the tongue.
Value. Isn't that what this is about? How much it costs us
living this way.
A magnetic pull on your arm
check your phone as your mouth starts forming an answer
for what, exactly, the trade-off for productivity is,
but that's just when the sprayers
and the muzak click on,
mist kale and broccoli to "Singing in the Rain"
and the voice of Gene Kelly saying *Stand still, hotshot.*
You're not going anywhere.
You know he's right because you're already
spread thin, over-thinking every possibility. Creativity,
liquid thought, that's what's sacrificed.
Conjured focus
spent on trivialities. It comes
like the forgotten arm that you're scrubbing the clean spot
in the kitchen's dark corner, going at it
with a toothbrush
when what you should be worried about
is that the dog dropped a deuce on the table, the one-two
rising in your stomach that, though you just looked,
you still don't know
how long you've fucking been here.
You should move on, but it's like halon, or the gas
in fire extinguishers that sucks the air
right out of everything.
It's like a car you're changing oil beneath
that's gone off its blocks and now compresses your chest
like a night terror, the fear fantasy
that grips you
where a jacked truck driver hurtling along route three

T-bones your girlfriend from her scooter,
cascading Italian metal and coal
down the highway.
Or, as the two of you go out for crab legs
you suddenly remember what it was that her mother said,
and as you turn to tell her your truck's bumper
sweeps a deer's legs
from under it and the body hurtles
through the front glass and into the passenger seat,
displacing her torso from where she sits.
How can you breathe
with this phone and all this goddamn black and white tile?
You can't. Even the cooler's cold air won't skulk away
the anxieties you never insulated
yourself against.
Every pill of trouble you've borrowed
against an astronomical monthly percentage rate.
So this is what it's like failing gloriously,
though at what eludes you.
Do we have enough eggs? Cartons stretch, infinite,
down the hallway of your mind. White ovals in corrugated boxes
placed between mirrors you peer between,
reflected forever. Process.
Choice. You're paralyzed in the place
feeling belongs. Why are you here, anyways? The volume
cranks to eleven on the muzak. *Who would do this
to me?* but even as you ask
you know. Eyes retreat into their orbits.
Your body, exhausted by the mind that dogs it. The sprayers
go at it again, and so does Gene Kelley,
cackling over the chorus.
People continue to split, flow around
the inaction you protect with a sword flaming at your
garden gates. What time is it?

FAILURE

yanks the logging chain his pet slipped his own neck into, then mashes his pink,
whiskery nose in it. *This is what he wants? Then this is how I'll give it to him.*
Charley the rat welcomes this hard knock motivation handed down like a knot
at the end of his generation, but which he doubles down on himself.

Volume and cadence. He believes impact is what'll get him there and so Charley
says nothing when Failure tears pages from *Pumping Iron* magazine,
Boris Vallejo covers ripped from dimestore Fantasy & Erotica. Magnetizes
the ragged pictures in a mural bordering a bare spot in the fridge's stainless,

mirror finish so when Charley slinks to his dish for watery gruel he sees tear-
purpled fur and his eyes surrounded by all that he isn't. On one torn page,
a string-clad Eros clings to Conan the Barbarian's leaden calf. Arm raised to
the lightning that meets it, an acrylic bulge of vein thunders over bicep

and broadsword. National Lampoon poster with only the barest fur
on Beverly D'Angelo, adoringly kneed before a hypertrophic Chevy Chase.
He mugs the camera as he thrusts a tennis racket up to the storm of sky. Conan,
or Clark Griswold—each a reminder of how easy it is falling short

of self-portraiture. This, the comparison Failure threatens us with until we believe
we're the diva worshipping, cock level, the mad tyrant kicking sand in our eyes
as beachgoers gather, guffaw our mosquito tits and lumpy butt, capellini triceps.
Better to forget what *plateau* means, and the law of diminishing returns,

how muscle ceases making gains when worked the same way twice.
Sometimes even I try unyoking myself but Failure's been calling the shots
so long he's not going to give it up. Laughs like a loon imitating a hyena.
Jerks the chain tighter, and this time when he smears my face in it

I come away with a bloody nose, accept my voice is too tinny
for barking orders, too shrill to even make the tryouts for *America's Got Talent*.
No such thing as a fifty-fifty relationship, just temporary mutual benefit
until someone commits a coup. I used him, now he uses me.

He's the one with the scissors. He's got the glue.

MONSTER

Blame instead the furies your nature divides into for how life saws in one
of two directions. Blame the sociopath glassed on pills, The Mothman,

or a cryptid not found in the genus of *homo*. One gibbous moon,
and you're a split quince. Halves fall from a lycanthrope's anatomy.

Lupine kidney beside human spleen. Blood greases the brass doorknob.
Culpable, who is? Take the orange pill and Big Pharma's credited

for the column of checks beside the maintenance sheets. Your truck's fluids
in cc's and liters on color-coded spreadsheets. Alphabetized, dated.

Take nothing, spend the day tracing patterns in the sponged ceiling tile,
and the drill sergeant ballpeens your lazy forehead because you're trafficking

in *his* fungible time, measuring your value by the metronome's swath.
Stay out late and tomorrow you'll pay, pound out extra miles. Truth is,

haters gonna hate, but every day with you's the same. Hand to lying mouth,
mouth to fool mind. Alibis. Eyewitness sketch of a baddie skulking

'round the hood everyone knows is you. You've got this. A man divided,
stitched together. A face made handsome by the boils on the other.

Man, you really have it in for yourself. Dualities from Siam and Las Vegas,
respectively, you try herding into the salon, expect they should do anything

but fight like tail-tied cats slung over the clothesline. Good luck with that.
In the age of fire codes and more resistive materials, your fireman

still needs an arsonist. Winnow all the dark out of the night
and something in the lighthouse is gonna break.

GHOST

Sometimes you're a burning house where the flame's long been kindling,
racing through the balloon frame's walls and rafters. Only it's hidden in the eaves
in a wavelength of light that can't be seen with the naked eye. No warning system chirps
lo batt, alarm. No blinking light. No klaxons or Class-Q warbles as scorched vinyl
oozes down the house like burnt marshmallow. Lacking the proper instruments
for detecting heat in the void spaces, no one even knows anything's wrong.
No neighbors gather outside the property's perimeter, shouting *Jonathan!
Come out!* Your name, in infrared, just visible through the wall.
A thermal imager's LCD indicates a drop in temperature
by white on black, a ghost between washout and jet, floating inside
a bathtub like a sensory deprivation chamber, a frog in a pot.
Sometimes you can separate. Stand in the brick-cobbled,
weed-cracked street. Sometimes you see through the wall like a sheet,
your shadow behind it, leeches curling from your dripping hair,
off-gassing, shimmery with heat,
lapping the night's star-black.

four

FISSION FOR DUMMIES

Reactions

Like a matchstick pyramid, only inverted: Slivered white pine slits in light. Red-capped cornices, paraffin and ammonium phosphate. One matchstick, struck at the peak, flares

Wavering, descends

A pinball caroms a rack of pinballs

A penny dimes a parabola into a mouse trap-filled room

A showering of hammers

Your neighbor's body, overwhelmed in its reaction to a bee sting

Cooling System

Veins, arteries in a closed circulatory system of *Good in, bad out*

Consider a car motor: excess heat from the thousands of controlled blasts per minute, exchanged in water pumped through the engine block's passages, to the radiator, cooled by finned air

Containment

Pool tables' bumpers. Rubber runners

Bitumen, lathing. Drywall and stucco for dermis

Two feet of steel. Six feet concrete

Hollow, graphite block

Failure

With no means for heat exchange, even carbon steel loses tensile strength

Concrete spalls

Carbon dioxide toxifies the lungs' alveoli like limp sacks of old grapes

Uranium shrapnels through thin fabrics. Tissues, skin.

PRIPYAT

Approach

An hour North of Kiev hardtack road frays to potholes and slush
at the Exclusion Zone. Where the drop gate designates the Russian-controlled,
thirty-kilometer perimeter Oksana calls the *Zone of Alienation*

a guard with a Ukrainian flag patched on his cossack and a german shepherd
stops us at the candy-striped bar. Black gloved, Kalashnikov
slung by a leather strap, he searches the van. Checks my passport

against a Xeroxed proof that I paid the two hundred dollar tour fee,
ten percent of which has reached him because he lets us in.
Cleared as benign, Oksana arrows the white van through forests

of new growth. Soon we'll reach Chernobyl Reactor No. 4.
Swerve. She narrowly dodges the wild boar which dart from the snowy
windrows of trees. Points, tells me the neat rows and columns

of young firs are headstones for 1986, buried ten feet down.
Burial mounds, but level where the Liquidators dug a basin wide enough
to consume the contaminated forest they bulldozed,

then covered with sand. It looks like a Christmas tree farm,
and I want to see it when she says some of them glow a hazy blue at night.
Many things she should not show me, but as the lip of No. 4 cooling tower's

wide rim emerges from the treeline like a milk bottle dusted in lead,
I know that she will.

Schoolhouse

See the door, torn mathematically from its jamb. Raw, gouged wood
bares signs of recent trauma. A teardrop wreath propped on a tripod just inside:
fake roses and white carnations, faded spruce bough like a pipe cleaner
bent in a circle. See the apothecary cabinet flung open, how it salts

the hallway's lathe floor with shattered decanters and dwarven,
elephant faces of gas masks. I enter where the hallway branches into the nursery,
see wire frames of double bunks crammed in the corner like shopping carts.
The plank floor burnt through in two places calculates sentiment

in a campfire of beer cartons, charred joists. It seems overdone.
Under a microscope nothing is as it seems. Anagrams drip spray paint
down the kindergarten room's mural wall. Beneath, I can see where sheaves
of lead paint fall away, a schoolboy in a blue uniform cap gazes upward,

a Soviet rocket seeming to rise behind him. A vandal with an eye for drama
has posed desks in neat rows that form an illusion of a shadow flash,
childrens' effigies painted on the wall. An orange, pastel chair
props up a rag doll fitted in a gas mask. Only the cubbies' metal doors,

I think, may be real. Their brushed, acrylic yellow still canary bright.
Dump truck, knobby tires. On another, a duck on wheels. There—
hummingbirds with human eyes circle a sunflower. Names scratched beneath,
a lover's tryst. Cyrillic characters over a heart, a mushroom cloud beneath.

Tired, as if from empathizing too much with a dramatic film,
I turn from the doctored, ruined layers of history, step down the hallway.
Careful, so nothing is contaminated, I exit the missing door outside,
into the honest witness of trees.

Forest Wormwood

From the van's window Oksana points the yellow detector at the skeletal
scotch pines and acacias *babushkas* sometimes call the *Black Forest, Red Forest*.
Ticking, the device ratchets to a chitter and the LCD shows forty sieverts,
which means we can't go there. What needles haven't fallen

from the whispy tree husks are brown and snow doesn't collect around
their trunks. She says the thickest limbs choke on plutonium,
that strontium-90 gingers the bark, curling it like wet paper. That iodine,
and cesium-127 rosin the conifers' xylem and phloem

hard as unlidded cans of red paint. I think of the cadavers I saw
in the Body Worlds exhibit in Chicago. Muscles and veins deflated of blood,
how they were injected with plastic so we could see statues of the living.
An article I read soon after about Harold McCluskey—*The Atomic Man*:

An explosion blasted his face with americium and bits of metal,
irradiating his body with five hundred times the maximum allowable dose,
and though he shouldn't have survived, the officials who came,
collected his body when he died years later insisted only *heart disease*.

Once more she waves the detector's reedy, faxing noise
toward the wraithlike pines, can't explain how it is they still stand.
The sluggish diesel whines beneath us as she drives into the land
of comic book origins. Hometown of giant lizards.

Waxhouse mannequins for the carnival.

Proximity

A bull moose feeds between two buildings that once housed
thirty-thousand workers and their families. We stand
in a doorway entrance at the ground level, unworried,
sure his rack's girth won't allow him entrance.

Alert now to our presence, he lips the fallen willow twigs
into his mouth. Oksana says wolves and even
the black bear have moved into the lonely nuclear city,
seem civil as people. Alone on one of the tenement's

upper floors where she often came to journal,
reclining on a sill, she occasionally watched the tame things
wandering where trees broadened over
the once-manicured lawns. She says it's not curiosity

or pride, but time and nearness that make us forget
what is truly dangerous. A window
on the third floor where her red hair blazed as she wheeled
to the white wolf like rolling thunder in the doorway.

Its lupine breath, penny rot. Ammonia as her bladder let go.
Face red, she turns to the moose, which raises its head.
Bored, he chuffs in our direction and lopes away.

ectopia cordis

A romantic lie, believing animals possess more than instinct.
A town crumbles in Chile, and your beagle forecasts earthquake weather,
the same warning she gives the bad UPS man in the brown truck. I don't know,
but I see the evidence in Kiev's Chernobyl museum. Desiccated in a glass case,
a golden retriever puppy with five inchoate, cloven paws. Two swine fetuses,
conjoined. Eighteen hours after the fourth meltdown expecting mothers
still craved pickles and potting soil. Babushkas divined from leaves
only signs of health and wealth for April twenty-six in their tarot deck,
rune stones skittered across card tables while gamma particles
settled into their beliefs and their unborn. Dismantling DNA,
relinking chains of code for breathing to code for walking.
Bare stumps and lungs exchanging features.
Boy-child with a raw heart beating on his chest
where just now you see your own. Shallow divots for eyes,
cataracts marbled as milk glass. Religious pundits say
Chernobyl Christians read *The Bible* wrong. It's time to pack it in
when even the weatherman isn't on your side.

Signs

Oksana says the smallest creatures
change most by what passes through them, to watch for signs.
Hirundo rustica—the brown barn swallow's feathers
blanch albino, counterfeiting hope. The purple spiderwort
blushes pink with radiation.

Point and Shoot

Red, encased in plastic, the Geiger counter is small enough
it fits my palm. The characters on its monochromatic LCD screen
like the elongated, hexagonal bars on any digital wristwatch.
Chittering, it reads my pulse. Stucco, biomass. Open air.
Everywhere I point the instrument increases its frequency and pitch
with sieverts, roentgens.

§

I am told not to snap pictures of the horror, instead only hold the Geiger counter
like a phone's camera towards it. And so I aim it at Forest Wormwood,
and I aim it at the ground where contamination has settled,

rising again through hard-packed tundra as *leachate*. I aim the instrument
at the unused ferris wheel bright as a sunflower petal's tips silvered in the nitrogen
of twenty-five years. I aim it at snow-caked bumper cars, post-collision.

I aim the instrument at the black-and-gray disaster monument where two hands
erupt, palming a reactor. I aim it at Reactor Four a hundred meters behind,
still leaking through its lead pores and rivets where the sarcophagus' panels

have fallen in. I aim it at the collie mutt Oksana calls *Cherny*, or *No. 4*,
ruffle his ears, then aim it at my hand to show I am afraid. I aim the instrument
at the Volkswagen rusting on a building's roof, diagonal on corner parapets.

At the highrises, mirroring each other but for the flags atop them. One banner:
A two-headed eagle. The other: red, waving a peasant's hammer and sickle.
I take aim at statues. At Marx's westward gaze, and at Lenin's lithified brainpan.

I aim the instrument in places I do not have permission to enter. I aim it
at the boxing ring, rotting, in the octagon room and at the busted safe on its side
in the sacked supermarket. But not at Fire Brigade No. 2. Not at the rolltop doors,

open on an empty bay. Not where the red pumpers and tenders belong,
gone now to Rassokha where they rot below ground. Not at pin-ups
of American supermodels now finding religion as their bodies continue failing them.

Skull-shaped hole in drywall. Vodka bottles heaped in the sub-floor
maintenance pit. I lower the instrument's accusing lens that won't change anything.
I'm done collecting mementos for pain. Here, my brothers who lived what those

who've never been jarred awake by the bell might call *work*. Neither do I aim it
at the monument to the firemen who died on April twenty-sixth. Not at the six
who traded themselves for the one-hundred and eighty others, and their countrymen.

I brace myself against the granite nozzle of the fireman closest the stone centerpiece
as if my weight could stay his blitz. Stone—what it means choosing this life,
formed now to forever rush into the black hazard of twisted rebar and drop ceilings.

Toward any flickering, billow, or plume. A muffled cry. Sparks in the night.
A reactor stack, in miniature.

The Liquidators

> *Objective: Slow fusion in the core to ascertain if residual heat is sufficient in vaporizing water into steam for operating the turbines in the event of a power outage*

White-uniformed engineers and control room operators in bonnets
raise glasses of *horilka*. A toast. Even the Acting Director sips cognac from a rocks glass
as water pumped from the Pripyat River cools the reactor core,
now drained to the minimum levels.
The Director orders the bypasses,
relief valves disabled as red, protective hoods are flipped from appropriate toggles,
safety traded for accuracy of data. The exercise begins and necessary personnel
monitor their green, monochromatic displays, needles in mineral oil
for a change in pressure or temperature, number of sieverts
produced during partial shutdown.
Needles quiver, then jump.
Overhead, the fluorescents begin flickering. Ice rattles in the Director's glass,
and a bone-shaking tremor powders the floor with sheetrock.

The drunk driver thinks he will beat the train. Does not.

That's how it happens, too fast for the Director to shout the order.
Too fast to scramble the engineers and operators in time to trigger actuators,
insert the retarding boron rods to slow the fusion
when the unexpected spike in demand for power indicates the reactor to increase output,
which it does in a cascade of heat which vaporizes the remaining water,
warping the rods so they cannot seat in the graphite block,
cannot slow the core's runaway reactions.
The world buckles at a point in the Ukraine.
Air, hoisted from the workers' throats when chambered steam mushrooms,
fractures ten feet of concrete and steel encasing the core.
Operators and engineers bottleneck in a heap at the door, trample one another
as they fail escaping the graphite-sleeved Promethean heart rupturing in a column of
rearranging elements—an erupting caldera which pancakes through the floors,
shrugs the forty-ton crane from the roof.

§

At Chernobyl Nuclear Power Station Fire Brigade No. 2,
Lieutenant Pravik thinks he only imagines the bottle of *Khortytsa*
clinking where the men hide it behind the stove.

That it is only his nerves singing with strong tea
at this late hour and this week's paycheck of rubles scattered
on the card table's brown vinyl. Every red drop of blood

beating through him says he should fold. That his wife
would be displeased when he comes home smelling of Viceroys,
cobalt eyes webbed and bloodshot. Hit, discard.

Vapors swirl in the kitchen air between Alexei and Pavlo.
*Last week I saw a red-eyed blackbird the size of a man hovering
above one of the reactors.* Pavlo, to Alexei:

I see myself tomorrow, hovering above your wife's beard.
Alexei bucks his chair to the wall and lunges into Pavlo
whose knees bend in a boxer's stance to meet him.

Pravik leaps to, then again hears the rattle of glass
against steel and just glimpses his last card fall to the floor,
face-up on a suicide king as he careens with their fighting

into the bay where Pavlo's skull—pincered in the other,
larger man's forearm and bicep—bashes through the plaster
as the fire station's bell and klaxon begin bleating.

§

Static and gravel bookend the location blaring over the station PA.
    We zip into our mechanic's suits, clamber into the old Soviet pumper.

Tonight's rotation: Vissgerdis, Engineer. He drives, so I ride
   in the Captain's seat. Soon, we skim away layers of night sky,

star-glare bright and clear as Easter bells at last week's service,
   their candelabrums' wicks scattering light over the pumper's waxed cab.

Thirty years of alarms and warnings, their warble a low voice
   which lulls and twines the blood, whispers me to sleep. Red, then white

smears of light accustom themselves in a quiet for stewards
   of the unchanging, rumbling toward what is customary and safe.

Our faces, lit in the instrument panel's jewel. Green, and blue,
   they light the way to a fault in the wiring or a trouble alarm's

burnt-out sensor. Glitter to glitter, the reactors ahead like ocean
   oil rigs whose industry made beautiful by night stars stippled to them,

V's hands at ten and two. Alexei and Pavlo in the jumpseats.
   Quiet, they've forgotten their violence. Twinkling. Dust to dust.

Whine of the Cummins diesel grinding through the transmission's
   gears. Smell of straw, burning. A glow, scumbling the night blue-black.

   §

*Station Two Brigade on scene. We're going to need Pripyat's
and Kiev Region's Brigades for mutual aid!*

Pravik radios local dispatch,
then like a color he's never seen before, recalls the training and equipment
they were promised but never received—*Nuclear, Biological,
and Chemical Response.* How to apply the principles
of *Time, Distance, and Shielding,*
Dam, Dike, Divert, or when to shelter-in-place.

Schematics for equipment shutdown.
The War Room for tabletop exercises where the brass
would position models of pumpers, tenders, and firefighters in molded plastic
between cooling towers and a pond's blue acrylic.

Bunker gear, masks. Airpacks.
Personal Protective Equipment the Chernobyl Fire Brigade
never received. Resources whose need Commander Leonid justified
but the Director never approved.

Pravik considers instead what he knows.
Names of buildings, layouts. Egresses. That he now sees a column of smoke
solid as lava blackening the night, striations of red flickering
like blisters rising in a failing section of hose.

That the Machine Hall beside Reactor Four
is the most vulnerable exposure. That when in absence of Plan A,
Plan B will always work. *Put the wet stuff on the red stuff.*
Crags fountain from the roof's caldera,
fireballs lobbing onto surrounding structures.

§

Alexei! Pavlo! String two lines and extra sections of hose into
the Machine Hall! Vissgerdis, give them water and meet me inside!
I grab a set of irons and throw open the steel doors on the East side,

then return where Pavlo, Alexei, and V hunch on their ankles,
waiting for me with charged lines at the South entrance. I take the doors
with the halligan's forked end, and take my place as we plunge into

the grainy smoke, filling our mouths now with a taste of burning metal
and numbness stitching across our bare faces. Steam hisses.
The smoke whitens, thins, and I see the burning bitumen like shards

of a meteorite named *Star Wormwood*, splintered off and cratering
the concrete floor. Pieces of graphite core, little phosphorus stars burning
through tar, pop and sputter with each blast of water,

spalling into smaller suns. *Pripyat Fire Brigade to Pravik from
Kiev Brigade. We have four pumpers, on scene. What are our orders?*
Thumbing the mic, I recall rate of depletion, our half-life in these conditions,

and the assurance in Newton's Second Law that there is no death,
just a changing of energy. *Put out Reactor Four or they're all going up!*
Some relief comes when Commander Leonid arrives,

assumes command from the roof of Reactor Three where he directs
extinguishment of five fires formed into tornados of their own weather.
I hear the count as he manages apparatus and their crews:

Engines and men from Kiev and Pripyat directed to form pumper relays—
a modern fireman's bucket brigade—sending us water from the cooling ponds.
I don't know how long it's been, how many breaths I've taken

in the steam-clouded room when V says my eyes have changed from blue
to rusted cast iron. I don't know the measure of product
we've straight-streamed between the pumps and control stations,

breathing in what flashes white along the edges, off-gasing and entering us
through our cotton clothes and skin as we move among rekindling hotpots.
Lieutenant Vladimir Pravik, this is Commander Leonid Telyatkinov.

From the radio, his voice comforts me as my arms fill with heavy elements
of fatigue. *Commander Leonid to Pravik's Guard.* It's not Leonid,
but my father's voice—lost, returning to me many years after his MiG

went down somewhere over the Dead Sea. I want to tell him how close I am
to extinguishment, that I will soon leave this place. I want to tell Pavlo,
V, and Alexei: *Keep flowing!* Again I hear him, as if through canvas:

Leonid, to Pravik. Thank you. My father says I've put a knock on it
and I respond with steam and smoke. I write his name in water.
In the silence I mouth *Thank you, that I am become a tool*

and not a weapon. I let the line slip, then fumble, fall toward it. Repeat.
This is Commander Leonid Telyatkinov to Lieutenant Vladimir Pravik
and his men. We thank you. The Ukraine thanks you. I repeat. Into the black.

NOTES

Liquidators were any of both civil and military personnel who were called upon to deal with consequences of the 1986 Chernobyl nuclear disaster.

In Memoriam to the firefighters who died responding to the explosion at Chernobyl Nuclear Power Plant

Chernobyl Nuclear Power Plant Brigade

Vladimir Pavlovych Pravik, Head Guard, 2nd paramilitary fire brigade
Leonid Petrovich Telyatkinov, Head of the 2nd paramilitary fire brigade (2004)

Pripyat Brigade

Vasyli Ivanovych Ignatenko, Squad commander, 6th Paramilitary Fire/Rescue Unit
Viktor Mykolayovych Kibenok, Head guard, 6th Paramilitary Fire/Rescue Unit
Vladimir Ivanovych Tishchura, Senior Firefighter, 6th Paramilitary Fire/Rescue Unit
Nikolai Ivanovych Titenok, Firefighter, 6th Paramilitary Fire/Rescue Unit
Nikolai Vasilievich Vashchuk, Squad commander, 6th Paramilitary Fire/Rescue Unit

five

EDUCATION

Side streets narrow as gangways, he scours the red light district
for someone like her. Someone who wears horn rim glasses, chooses

books for him. Tells him, *Read to me aloud* as she goes down.
Desperate. Wounds still fresh, he scans the streets for a mistress,

whose flint-eyed instruction he will mistake for lover's writ.
Red blares down cobblestone alleys, billboards promising a salve

for loneliness. His lips, dry. Numb as he remembers them laboring,
forming, fishmouthing the Giving Tree's gifts he savored

as he savored her tongue's felt tip tracing his ilia in apogees of tension
and restriction, trailing to the sparse scree of hair at his cock's base.

Victoria! He stutters over the apples, the little boy needing always
just one more blessed thing. Before release, her mouth stops

and he says he loves her again. Our hero meets aureolas before eyes
of the women who own them, elevating their plush a few inches

so he must choose between neon and heaven, a quick tug or the pull
away that might make him larger than his hurt. Cornflower lace panties,

the blonde waif that fingers him in. I almost want that he bleed,
scrape his scar, and stay this shade of precious forever. I almost want

him to go face first against glass, tripping as he rises to meet
the impossible body of the prostitute who can not reenact his memories

of a second-grade teacher, lessons of stricture and withheld pleasure.
Watch now as she draws the purple window curtain. See her open

the armoire, walnut veneer. Unpack her tools. Boxes of tissues, gloves.
An assortment of pump bottles. Spermicide, lubrication,

in Hypoallergenic Blue, Latex White. See the dental dams rubber-
banded in a roll. Green. Watch her wash, tell him of her sisters,

how she misses them. Ukraine's poverty.
When she says her name, watch his heart stiffen also.

BLUE CHAPEL, BLUE CEMETERY

Ukraine's snowy countryside blinks by the train car
in a monochrome blear
until the color of the church throbs into sight.

You note the blue walkway and the flagstones,
set in an even camber toward the doors caked in blue paint,
ten feet high.
The fat, blue dome like a fallen teardrop
tapered to a needle's point.

Who doesn't think the strange means something
if only because he is there to see it?

The fence's perimeter, cobalt.
A wash of cornflower headstones muffled in snow,
cerulean moon.

You ruin this picture by making it yours.
Journaling, your speaker attaches allegory to blue's tired convention,
the scene's shading indicating your Seasonal Affective Disorder,
or aimless melancholia.

Blaming this country for your crime,
any presence trawls away from the simple,
strange blue church in a blue graveyard.

Look again: A glowing copse of trees
smears its ghost light alongside the speeding train.
Look again at the snow.
Blue.

Let a tiding of magpies remain a tiding of magpies.
Let your absence be a window.
Sometimes it is enough.

PETITION

Already fading is the blue church and blue graveyard,
myths of trees glowing like swamp gas the train gallops me away from.
I don't know if it was real. Still,

the memory honeys me to children's stories
couched with moral lessons in duty like the lantern of an anglerfish,
or St. Elmo's light, luring lost sailors to the stony shore.

Had I stayed home, would I disbelieve the wonders
I cannot explain? As a child, illustrating stories of Arthur and his knights
with crayons, I may as well have inked holiness in those eyes,

believing every story into parable, parable into gospel
he studied like manuals for gallantry. By day I wanted that flawlessness
gleam from my wooden sword as Sir Galahad the Pure,

that—like Sir Gawain—I might be Defender of the Poor,
and of Women. I wanted a need for worlds to save, fires to extinguish,
so I asked for a burr cut so my head might fit

the child's green bucket with holes visored in cellophane
and the bucket's bottom in hopes a diadem of light would appear above it.
By dark, mantled in the stars and moons of sheets,

I wanted a magician's judicious nature. I wanted so much
it seemed twenty-four hours a day want thrummed such a fever in my head
I could have split like a hot stone.

Swaying along the tracks, I can no longer tell how far I am
from there, only that the distance always widens. I have no requests for
celestial bigwigs by this open window

as I breathe particles of Hobbs and my Mother,
memories of carbon and the long-necked brontosaur. Open air asks nothing
to fill it, so neither do I, illumined in a path of light that long ago

received word that its star has died, but travels still.
This train car is a buoy for movement, and pines passing outside blur
their living across me.

ADDICTION TRACT

Children's coloring books teach us
to find *What is Missing?* from one of two similar pictures,
so I consider what was never there: Tonguing the molar's pith
which jags my jaw with each toggle.
Rubbernecking movements of illegals over
the US/Mexico border into Arizona, then reporting coordinates.
Conflict tours in which hummingbird wings throb
within my chest as I peruse galleries always of someone else's pain.
Oksana—my tour guide's red hair, burning deeper
as we wandered Chernobyl's *via dolorosas,*
describing for me the taste of radiation sickness
the way my Mother did her chemo treatments—
stuffed straw burning at the throat's back.

No, this itemized list has nothing on me.
Nothing of owning one's accomplishments long after the drugs
have left the building. Nothing of mental steroids,
or how electric emotions are, returning
after the jaw is locked so long, doubling you over
with their arrival. All I see's the same over-the-counter hang-ups
you get at any One-Stop liquor store, or doctor's office.
Support groups for bad behaviour, pills.
Compulsive sex. Addiction to avatars in virtual,
social networks. Flipping the tract over
so I see if I've missed anything, I still can't find
the right synonym, or what it means. Voyeurism.
Schadenfreude. The pain of others.

PAIN OF OTHERS

Heading home from the airport I find what was missing
from the pamphlet of addictions. A wreck on the fast lane's shoulder,
bad. Orange cones shunt the eastbound icy lanes together,
traffic at a crawl. Drawing attention if only
so we can look away, rescue trucks pincer the scene. Wigwags,
strobes. Gold leaf letters dime flash the towns they hail from
in headlights of passing vehicles. I look.
See the Wal-Mart box trailer, tumbled and split in the wide,
grassy median, a superstore's detritus burst from its riveted seams
like confetti. Millimeters-thin televisions

corrugated in plastic. Dolls, ripped from pink packaging,
dismembered likenesses of limbs flung ahead where fire trucks stage,
protect victims and firefighters in case the cones fail. I look again.
I don't want to, but I do, say it's so I can
reconstruct events as if understanding the past ever changes anything.
The driver of the diesel tractor must have used his air brakes
on the layer of snow scrimming the highway,
then jack-knifed, kingpin uncoupling from the truck's receiver
even as the trailer came around. Unburdened, but over-torqued, the semi
grabbed cinders, and dished the median, so moments later

the white Mazda3 torpedoed the truck's grill
on the driver's last living thought as she entered what looked to her
like a wolf's throat. *I hope he makes it home safe.* Motoring fills
the dusk, unpuzzled now before me.
I steel myself against blinding quartz lights on tripods, strung to
generators and the lead man's directives. I inch by, face set firm in my
prejudice that the victim must be a woman. Stop.
Again steel myself against the fear that's always there, that this time
I'll glimpse the face I know entangled with sheet metal, paint,
and flecks of nothing at all like rust.

This Plinko life of random prizes, then catastrophic loss.
Trauma, impartial to merit, or a boy I knew
who screamed *I AM! I AM! FUCK YOU, I AM!* swaying on his rooftop
from fury and too much scotch, falling seventeen rungs
to the boxwood elders. All these thorns I've dodged like big,
dumb meteorites falling from the sky as if on parachutes,
but will crater, then splash molten stuff
onto someone near me. Fryman, Knabe. Mason,
Alexander. My fire department brothers, their names I append
in DayGlo to the first responders' backs helping the victims,

their effectiveness comes in knowing one day
it might be their sons, wives pinned or pierced behind the A post,
beyond the hardened Nader bolt. I wish I were as wrong about
their methods as I am about their affliction:
Recognizing a blue feather braided like steel into the straight,
blonde hair, or the driver's chipped front tooth, its enamelled surface
he could map if asked—it's not her. But, no.
They all are. Someone's *her*, separated from my only by
circumstance, a thin scrap of time and place, and physics' second
law of dying between two metal bodies.

Traffic moving, I feather the accelerator
as if an egg nested beneath. Hear myself in my grandfather's voice
ask myself where I get off that I have time for carving poems.
How long can this privilege last? I confess:
Sometimes I'm so afraid of flying my lungs forget they're life support
for a fool. One wrong move and dead is dead in any-numbered
world. Ionizing radiation. Leg scraped by uncovered screw.
Later, tetanus. Maybe infection sprints
a red line to your heart. So many snares between night's
spatial drift and gasping awake you can't hardly move

without getting some on you. Wave a UV light
over all this dust and see a glowing patchwork of scars. Reader,
remember your conflict tours as you pass other people's wrecked lives,
saying to yourself *at least that's not me*, or,
*at least that's not my someone trapped, bleeding as the golden hour
slips away*. We're lucky, you and I. We know just how good we've got it.
I speed from the accident scene, call the only parent left
because I haven't today heard his deep,
comforting baritone and then I call my partner whom I love
because of how hard she tries loving me.

Tonight, friends roll cigarettes, drink dark beer
in the garage and a timbre just below sinuous, from wood-turning
to motorcycles, ending in the key of gratitude. Ending with brothers.
Fire Department, Air Force. Human brothers
we sometimes love to hate, others hate loving. My one, true brother
in Germany I haven't talked to in years, but miss so badly I wipe
tears from the space bar with every revision.
We have everything and nothing is taken we don't freely give.
The clamminess in my palms when taking off or landing
reminds me of my relative safety.

Each time wheels separate from earth
or grab tarmac I know roulette's golden triangle has passed me by.
Then, the bone-swelling feeling of lightness until I'm many-
tongued and feverous with gratitude.
The Serenity Prayer I mouth for the sad tie beside me
who says every second after eighteen is one in which we are dying.
I turn, face the fact of him, but not him, then say in the words
of the living: *Thank you. I look beyond this blessed wing,
see more comfort than pain. Thank you. Every moment,
every breath left in me is Thank You.*

ACKNOWLEDGEMENTS

Thank you to poets Lesley Brower & Emily Rose Cole for your friendship as much as your editing skills throughout the arrangement and revision process.

Thank you to longtime friends & colleagues Steve Falcone, Joanna Christopher, Adam Tarrants, David Mason, Lance Liggett, and Ron Clark.

Also to Brock Musoiu, Jennifer Musoiu, Vanessa Travelstead-Marchal, Jarrod Travelstead, Heidi Kocher, & the Nelson family.

Thank you again to Cobalt Press.

ABOUT THE AUTHOR

Jonathan Travelstead served in the Air Force National Guard for six years as a firefighter and currently works as a full-time firefighter for the city of Murphysboro, and also as co-editor for *Cobalt Review*. Having finished his MFA at Southern Illinois University of Carbondale, he also turns a lathe, crafting pens under the name Scorched Ink Penturning. His first collection *How We Bury Our Dead* by Cobalt Press was released in March 2015.

PUBLICATIONS FROM CONFLICT TOURS

Barking Sycamores (2014): "Pleasure Principle (Pitbull Pills)", and "Symbiosis"
Blinders Literary Journal (Winter 2015): "Pripyat: Proximity"
Blue Lyra Review (Spring 2015): "Analysis Paralysis"
The Boiler Journal (Spring 2015): "Pain of Others"
Border Senses (Summer 2015): "After a Tooth Extraction, Zen"
Broad River Review (2013): "Border Patrol: Money Tree"
Cahaba Literary Journal (Spring 2015): "Ghost", and "Sentimental"
Festival Writer (January 2015): "Symbiosis"
Four Quarters Magazine (Winter 2015): "Signs"
HEArt Online (Summer 2014): "Riding the Beast"
Kudzu Review (Winter 2015): "Point and Shoot"
Marathon Literary Review (Winter 2015): "ectopia cordis"
Masque and Spectacle (2015): "Addiction Tract", and "The Scientist"
New Southerner (December 2014): "Letter to the Unborn"
New Verse News (Fall 2014): "Border Patrol: In-Processing", and "Corvids"
Off the Coast: "Fission for Dummies", and "Pripyat: Approach"
Oneiric Moor (Spring 2015): reprints of "Blue Chapel, Blue Cemetery", and "Addiction Tract"
pacificREVIEW (Spring 2015): "Schoolhouse"
Proximity Magazine: "Cartography", "Comfort", "Ridgerunner", "Trail Names", and Walasi-Yi Shoe Tree". Fall, 2014
Puff Puff Magazine: "Complicated" (Winter 2015); "Rapture" (Spring 2015)
The Quotable (Fall 2014): "For Clothes"
Really Systems (Fall 2014): "Myopia"
Red Paint Hill (Spring 2015): "Ultralight"
Red Wolf Journal (Fall 2014): "Cartography"
riverSedge (Spring 2015): "Monster"
saltfront (Winter 2015): "The Liquidators"
Southern Poetry Anthology, Volume VIII (Fall 2015/Winter 2016): Texas: "Coyote", and "Sonoran Desert, Warning by Rancher".
Star 82 Review (Winter 2014): "Tourist"

Still: the Journal (February 2015): "Petition", "Pripyat: Forest Wormwood", and "Rapture"
Two Hawks Quarterly (Spring 2015): "Signs"
Watershed Review (Spring 2015): "Education"
We Said Go Travel! (July 2014): "Field Worker"
Wildage Press (2015): "Blue Chapel, Blue Cemetery"
Wild Quarterly (May 2014): "Coyote", "Flat Tire on San Miguel Road, Met by Two Wild Horses", "Injunction", and "Sonoran Desert, Warning By Rancher"

AWARDS

New Southerner finalist (2014): "Letter to the Unborn"
Broad River Review Award finalist (2013): "Border Patrol: Money Tree"

www.ingramcontent.com/pod-product-compliance
Lightning Source LLC
Chambersburg PA
CBHW021446080526
44588CB00009B/718